COLUMBIA, The Street

How Five Kids Drove Their Parents and Neighbors Crazy

By Dr. James R. Gregory, With Richard Gregory, Bruce Gregory, and Wayne Gregory

Dedicated to Doris, our sister
who was taken from us too soon.

ACKNOWLEDGEMENTS

First and foremost, I wish to thank my wife, Evelyn, who indulges my many forays into the unknown with great humor, abiding encouragement, and love.

My longstanding and trusted editor, Linda Freeman, is not only a dear friend from college but also is married to my terrific friend from high school, Blake Freeman, who tolerates my continuing requests for Linda's time and attention. Should you find any grammatical or factual errors in this book, don't hesitate to get in touch with Linda Freeman (or Blake).

My brothers came through with an abundant number of contributions that made this book a labor of love and appreciation for our wonderful upbringing. I'm so thankful that they didn't kill me when they had the chance.

Peter Miserendino has been my go-to illustrator for decades. Pete always understands my requests despite getting minimal direction. Should you ever need a first-class illustrator, I highly recommend Pete, who can be reached at Pete@ptpie.com.

I also want to acknowledge our two grandchildren, Charlotte, and Maxwell, who bring great joy to our lives and keep me young at heart. I try to instill in them the spirit of creative adventure nurtured in me by my upbringing.

My Universe

Columbia Street was my universe in the 1950s. It is a thinly asphalted dead-end street about 300 feet in length and sloping downhill past my house to the bottom where, before cul-de-sacs were fashionable, the road just stopped at a row of pine trees. The best feature about Columbia Street is that it had a substantial continuous slope to it which was perfect for sled riding in winter or crate racing in the summer. The starting point for any race was our driveway where the relatively uninterrupted crack across the asphalt was perfect for a starting line. I learned later that Columbia Street extended about a half-mile up the hill, but the section where I lived when I was little was my only concern. In a neighborhood called Berkley Hills, Columbia Street was a working-class community in the small, historic town of Johnstown, Pennsylvania.

My dad had an important job with the steel mill where he was a heater in the rolling mill. The 1950s and 60s were optimistic years where everything was an opportunity to be explored, and almost everyone was a friend. I have a Norman Rockwell vision of my early life and see most everything from that time in sepia colors like the kind of photographs taken with my mother's old box camera. Things were perfect unless there was a strike at the mill, and then things were not so good.

The Caboose

I was the youngest of five kids. My sister, Doris, was primarily out of the house when I was old enough to know her. She had gone to nursing school, and I remember her as being very pretty. When Doris was babysitting me, she would play the clarinet and sometimes sing jazz when I was the only audience who could appreciate her beautiful voice. She also smoked cigarettes which would take her life at a young age. My brother Dick, as I remember him, was a tough guy. He was mechanically inclined and sometimes had grease under his fingernails from working on engines. He went into the Navy and was deployed for long periods. Later, when I was in high school, he started a business and hired me to deliver his machines around town in a tan Volkswagen bug. This required his teaching me to use a stick shift, and without either of us realizing it, he became my mentor for entrepreneurship as well. Next came my identical twin brothers, Wayne and Bruce (in that order). They ruled the roost in our family during my tenure. They focused on themselves, and everyone focused on them. The twins were into basketball and football, so that meant we often went to their practices and always went to their games. Bruce, at 6'2", was several inches taller than Wayne, so most games and discussions were around his efforts of playing varsity, although I always enjoyed watching Wayne play on JV because he just seemed to be a little more relaxed about sports.

Since there was a six-year difference between the twins and me, I was "the caboose" or the "afterthought," but never the "mistake"; at least, no one said that out loud. In my baby scrapbook, I have noticed how proud my parents seemed to be of me. My dad wrote in my scrapbook, "Jimmy is the best baby in all America, and Russia, too."

Jimmy sitting in his little white rocker flanked by the twins.

I certainly felt special. I was often called "The Teddy Snow Crop Baby", a name inspired by a cute little teddy bear mascot used in 1950s commercials for Snow Crop brand frozen foods. Since I never had to worry about being loved, as the "youngest in the family," I savored all the benefits that came with the title of being the youngest in the family. After being bathed and made to look fresh in a white terry cloth bathrobe while holding my teddy bear, I would settle myself on my vinyl-covered rocker on Sunday nights to watch Sid Caesar and Imogene Coca who performed on the *Your Show of Shows* or *Ed Sullivan*.

Bruce and Wayne had wedge shaped pillows, so they could lie on the floor to watch TV, and one evening when my brother Wayne was lying on his pillow watching a western, a character in the program was pistol-whipped. Then, according to Wayne, "The next thing I knew, Jimmy hit me on the head with his cap gun so hard that I do not remember the rest of the TV program."

Jimmy checking his siblings for soft spots.

A Great Insult and Better Response

Doris was mischievous, to say the least. One time, Dick and Doris were wrestling, and
she got on top of Dick, holding his hands down. Right above his face, she started a saliva spit that would descend right before the crucial moment when she would suck it back. Doris ignored Dick's protests as she continued her creative torture. Finally, gravity overcame her skills, and Dick received this gravest of insults. Dick's anger supplied him with superhuman strength, and he threw her off and chased her up the stairs to the bathroom. Just as he reached for the handle, Dick heard the latch click, and, despite Dick' protested threats, Doris thought

11

she was safe. Dick then got an idea and went up to the attic. He climbed out onto the roof and carefully squirmed down to the porch roof where there was a bathroom window. Doris sat there like royalty on the closed toilet seat smoking a smuggled cigarette. When she went to blow her puff out the window crack, she was shocked and startled to see Dick's face at the window. Dick got the last laugh. More importantly, Doris knew that she wasn't safe in any room of the house!

The Magic of Christmas

To say that Christmas at the Gregory residence on Columbia Street was magical doesn't do it justice. My father had a specific point of view about how Christmas morning should play out, and it didn't matter what kind of effort it took or how late he stayed up on Christmas Eve. He would make sure it worked, choreographing the event like the Radio City Music Hall Christmas Show. The only advanced preparation visible to the family was the setting up of the undecorated Christmas tree. After we kids went to bed, Santa and Mrs. Claus set to work decorating the tree and assembling the presents to maximize the impression the whole splendid scene would make in the morning.

The stockings were hung (by the fake cardboard fireplace) with care!

Everyone conspired to make sure they supported the storyline and the main character so that I would be convinced of Santa's visit. I was usually the first one awake on Christmas morning, so I would awaken all the others. We would gather at the top of the steps, giggling and pushing, while my dad would go down to the living room to turn on the Christmas tree lights.

We kids would all try to sneak a peek at the presents, but once the lights were on, we rushed downstairs, making an obligatory stop to ogle at the magnificent glittering tree and then onto the gifts.

We were not a wealthy family, but I didn't know that because my parents went all out at Christmas to find us anything we wanted. How they kept the presents hidden until Christmas morning remains one of the great mysteries of the universe.

All these Christmas festivities had two unintended consequences. I believed in Santa Claus longer than I should have, and my belief was so strong that when I realized it was an illusion, it tended to disillusion me from being able to have a total commitment to essential building blocks in the future. For example, while I went to church with my mom, I was skeptical about giving it my full belief and support of its teachings. The same was true for personal relationships; while I enjoyed them, it took a long time to commit to them. I'm not critical of my upbringing and wouldn't trade it for any other, but even the purest of intentions can sometimes have an unintended repercussion.

Traditions

A fascinating Christmas tradition at our home was having a breakfast of salt mackerel, a fish that came soaked in a brine of salt and preserved in wooden kegs.. This tradition must have come down from prior generations because we never discussed the convention – it just existed. Fixing the salt mackerel for consumption took days of preparation. The fish had to be removed from the kegs and put into a large pan filled with freshwater. The oily salt would seep out, and the fresh water had to be exchanged several times a day until it was determined that the fish was fit to cook.

The mackerel was then slowly boiled in a frying pan, and then one fish, a thick piece of homemade bread, fresh butter, and ketchup was served to each person. A cup of coffee, even to those at a young age, seemed to go well with this special Christmas breakfast. The meat was coaxed out of the bony fish with an upside-down fork, and when a substantial lump of the mackerel flakes was ready, the scoop was placed carefully on the buttered bread and eaten. Oh, my goodness! What a unique and delicious taste. Somehow, that seemed the perfect way to celebrate Christmas morning.

Not everyone fully appreciated this tradition, and it was somewhat of a rite of passage for new members of the Gregory Clan. One aunt by marriage who visited our house on

Christmas Day carried along a bottle of Airwick next to her nose. We all thought that was pretty funny, but my dad didn't see the humor.

Colorado Blue Spruce

Another Christmas tradition was the annual search for a perfect Colorado Blue Spruce. Once the tree was selected, my dad and oldest brother Dick would then dig it out by the roots, wrap it in burlap, and then put it in a tub of water outside until Christmas Eve when the cumbersome tree would be carried into the house for decoration. After Christmas, the tree would then be stored on the porch until spring when it would be carried outside and planted in the yard. My family did this until they ran out of room in the yard to grow these huge trees.

Our home on Columbia Street. The trees in the yard were once Christmas trees in the living room.

The Great Leveling Project

When my parents moved in 1941 into our house on Columbia Street, they resolved to have a flat yard and enough attractions to keep their children close to home. True to its name, the neighborhood was called Berkley Hills for the excellent reason that any level property was non-existent. When our dad had made up his mind to do something, he would accomplish the task, no matter the effort. This particular project took a decade of work to achieve the goal of a flat yard. First, Pop and my brother Dick dug off the 12 inches of topsoil and moved it by wheelbarrow to a soil pile for later use. It took years for this phase alone. After that, the yard had to be raised by hauling hundreds of loads of fill dirt that a bulldozer would spread to make level. Dad used a 5-ton dump truck and hauled many loads of dirt from the Moxham district's Cypress Avenue Elementary School, an elementary school that was expanded and converted to University of Pittsburgh at Johnstown's first building and campus. (In one instance, the bed of the dump truck became stuck in the air when the load failed to pour out of the bed as it was being dumped.) Lastly, the bulldozer spread the original collected topsoil as the top layer.

One dump truck got stuck up in the air when his load failed to dump.

The Great Dry Wall Project

The great leveling project needed a retaining wall to hold the vast amount of fill dirt hauled into the yard. So, we kids were put to work helping a neighbor dismantle a rock garden and its wall and carrying away the stones in our little wagon to where the drywall was to be located. Dick made a game out of everything, and he pretended the wagon was a large dump truck with a powerful engine. Dick would pull the wagon, and Bruce and Wayne would push. They would run over the same path until it had made visible grooves in the dirt. Since I was too young to participate, I enjoyed watching.

The Great Sewer Project

After years of work in creating the drywall and finally leveling the yard, we were notified from the municipality that we needed to connect with the new sanitary sewer system that was installed in the neighborhood. Pop had to hire a backhoe to dig a six-foot-deep hole the length of our now perfectly flat yard. We treated the whole event as an adventure and pretended that we were now into trench warfare of WWI, but that escapade was short-lived when our safety-conscious father said that using the trench for playing was verboten. When the ceramic pipe was installed, the tough job began of replacing the soil in the ditch, so every day after school, we were assigned to fill in at least 6 feet of the trench. On a positive note, the sewer line allowed Pop to install a much-needed "extra" toilet in the basement which, by the way, had the coldest toilet seat in America.

This photograph was taken about the time that the sewer trench was put into the backyard. Dick was home on leave from the service, and the twins were dressed up for some occasion. I managed to photobomb the picture in the lower left.

Building a Playground

After the yard was finally level, Dad decided he would turn our yard into a playground in order to keep us kids close to home. I remember pleasantly several designs that never made it to the production phase. However, we had a merry-go-round that was a lot of fun but came with safety concerns such as that of a kid's becoming entangled inside of the spinning circle. However, it evolved over time and was an ingenious design.

20

There was also a teeter-totter made of wood that could be turned on its side and converted to an instant fort for war games. Dad also designed our two adjustable oak chaise lounges, extremely heavy devices that made a distinctive wood-on-wood sound when rolled from place-to-place. The homemade swing set with basketball backboard was a much-used addition to the backyard. Bruce had a hand in making sure that the hoop was an official height – ten feet from hoop to the ground. Every inch of every homemade contraption had to be safety proofed. Bending over all sharp edges and checking for stability against tipping were standard procedures.

A glimpse of our flat backyard. The twins were in Little League. I was imitating them.

War Games

We all played war games in the backyard. For my
brother Dick, it was the Second World War, and the venue was
always Guadalcanal. The elderberry bushes beyond our stone
wall made the perfect jungle canopy, and the soil was
conducive for digging foxholes. One particular foxhole grew
until it became an underground bunker large enough for us to
stand up in, but you have to remember that we were a bit
shorter then. The top was covered with logs and branches,
leaving a small hole uncovered for access. The clay was moist
and compacted nicely into hand-sized hand grenades. After
manufacturing an adequate quantity, for some reason, we
decided to attack our neighbor Mrs. B's house and left the mud
grenades decorating the side of her house. Mom immediately
ran out on the porch and yelled for us to leave Mrs. B's house
out of the fighting. Apparently, they were a nonaligned
country.

Playing Army in our backyard Bruce, cousin Barry, cousin David, and Wayne.

General Jimmy being saluted by his soldiers. Notice the white gun made of solid wood.

A Room Full of Strangers

Despite my confidence of being loved, one of my earliest memories as a toddler was a fear of abandonment I experienced after becoming separated from my parents. They had taken me along to an open-house tour of a new elementary school built for our area's children, and I had temporarily become separated from them. I was suddenly in a room full of strangers and immediately became panic-stricken with no idea of what to do. It couldn't have been more than two minutes before my folks realized that I was not with them and immediately returned to find me. Everything was fine, except those couple of minutes were alarming.

Today, my four-year-old grandson asked me to take him to the bathroom at our home and then asked me to make sure no monsters were lurking inside. Then, while he did his business, he asked me to talk to him from outside the door of the bathroom to make sure I wouldn't abandon him while he was using the toilet. I understood exactly where he was coming from and happily stood guard for him.

My First Touchdown

Since there was a six-year age gap between my twin brothers and me and another six-year gap between the twins and my older brother, we never really had the opportunity for family sports to be played by the Gregory siblings. So, while my brothers played on school teams, I was only allowed to watch from a distance.

Once, while my dad was driving home from my brother's football practice, I saw a magical event going on in my neighborhood. Some of the older kids decided to have a pickup football game in their yard, and I was thrilled to see such a vibrant undertaking so close to our home. I asked my dad if I could play, and he said that it would be up to the other kids who were already playing. After parking the car in our garage, Dad and I walked to where this impromptu game was taking place, and after watching these older kids play a couple of downs, my father asked if they would mind allowing Jimmy to play for a little while. Reluctantly, they agreed and were determined to be good sports when they decided to hike the ball to me on the first down. Of course, I had no idea what to do because all I knew was that I had the ball, and I needed to start running for all I was worth. Unfortunately, I was running the wrong way. I heard my team yelling what I thought were words of encouragement, but when I crossed the goal, both teams looked at me with disgust. This was a mystery to me because I thought the idea was to cross the goal line with the ball, which I had done. My dad said, "OK, Jimmy, time to go." None of the kids came to my defense, and my father provided no further explanation.

Over dinner that night, I proudly told my brothers that I scored my first touchdown in a football game at our neighbor's yard. They asked my dad if that was true, and he responded affirmatively with a modest shake of the head. It was only then that I learned the finer points of the game. Luckily, memories were short in those days, and soon I was reinstated in our neighborhood football league's hierarchy.

Cousin Karen

Karen Senior is my first cousin and a month younger than I. She continues to live in nearby Windber, which is a small town located in southwestern Pennsylvania that's even smaller than Johnstown. She meant the world to me when we were children and getting together with her was the highlight of my week. Of course, we were usually arguing within five minutes of her arrival.

Cousin Karen and Jimmy enjoying refreshments in our backyard.

White Rabbits

I don't remember asking for white angora rabbits, but somehow the two female white rabbits my dad purchased became my responsibility. Pop built a pretty neat hutch for them, and the rabbits seemed to enjoy their new home. I had to feed and water them once in the morning and then make sure they had water late in the afternoon. I also had to shovel their poop from under the hutch. I wasn't a math whiz, but I had calculated those rabbits pooped roughly twice as much as they ate, or so it seemed.

I occasionally took them out of the hutch to eat fresh grass, especially if the neighborhood girls wanted to see them. The rabbits were cute with their pink eyes and ears and soft white fur, but they were not friendly or interactive whatsoever. They could scratch the heck out of you if you weren't careful when picking them up. One thing everyone agreed on was that these were huge, well-fed rabbits!

It didn't take long to learn that the two female rabbits were a heterosexual couple. One snowy morning, I discovered a tiny newborn bunny frozen between the inner box of the hutch the wire around the outside. I pulled it out, ran back to the house, showed it to my mother, and asked if she could save it. The baby was stiff as a board, but my mom promised she would try to nurse it back to health while I was at school.

By the time I got home, my dad had pulled out the hutch's inner box with all the babies and made a new larger hutch that would temporarily reside in our basement. We now had 12 rabbits, and by late spring, that number had doubled. As I began making multiple trips to feed them, the shoveling out the poop became a bigger and bigger burden. Raising rabbits wasn't fun at all. We couldn't give the rabbits away, so my dad solved the entire problem one day when I was at school by taking the rabbits to a farm. I asked if we could visit them, and he assured me we could. However, time passed, and I soon forgot about the rabbits.

Jimmy's white rabbits and the Beamer kids, Larry, Barry, and Lorraine.

Lil'Whisk

There was a vast Blue Spruce tree at the corner of an
adjoining street. All the older local kids would gather under it
to play cards or to hide from parents. When I first heard the
name "Lil'Whisk", I didn't think the older boy under the tree
who said the name was talking to me. Then to reconfirm that
there was no mistake, Earl repeated it, saying, "Jimmy, you are
Lil'Whisk." I was dumbfounded. It didn't make any sense, but
suddenly everyone was calling me Lil'Whisk. Just like that, I
had a nickname assigned without my involvement or approval.
I felt kind of privileged that my acquaintances thought enough
of me to create this name, even if I didn't know what it meant.

One day, my brother Dick was nearby, and I heard
someone yell, "Hey, BigWhisk!" OK, now the "Lil" part made
more sense. Later, at dinner that night, I asked my brother what
"BigWhisk" meant? He responded that whisk was short for
whiskers. He preferred the nickname *Greg,* but some friends
started calling him *whiskers*, and it stuck. He had heard the
boys calling me Lil'Whisk, and he thought that was pretty neat.
After that, I was happy to have the handle, but as these things
go, it was short-lived, maybe lasting through the summer until
they dropped it.

Little Whisk and Big Whisk discuss personal branding! Jimmy was never a slave to fashion as you can tell from his trousers!

Old Poker Face

While on the subject of nicknames, the same Blue Spruce was the venue for serious poker games. We gambled our lunch money every morning, weather permitting, while waiting for the school bus to arrive. One morning, Randy was dealt a straight flush, the highest possible hand you can get. Now, Randy was supposed to lose his lunch money, not win ours away from us, but today, he somehow had been dealt this unbeatable set of cards. Luckily for us, Randy was so beside himself with his good fortune that his face flushed, his eyes rolled, he blurted out, "Oh my Gawd! I can't believe it!" And then, to punctuate the situation, he proceeded to pee in his pants. Everyone thought he was bluffing until he wet himself,

31

at which point, all the players wisely dropped out of the hand. The chances of being dealt a straight flush are one in a million. The chances of misplaying a perfect hand were even-odds in this sad group. Randy was thereafter known as "Old Poker Face."

Soap Box Derby

The inspiration was a *Boys' Life* article that featured the year's national winners of the *Soap Box Derby*. The cars in the article looked beautiful with each vehicle proudly displaying its handsomely crafted hood and a number stenciled on its back panel. The cockpit had an actual steering wheel and an effective braking system, and the drivers were kids, maybe a year or two older than us. They were supported by a pit crew wearing shirts that had the same number as the car they sustained. How lucky these kids were to have the whole family involved in the sport!

When we finished reading the article, the six friends had agreed to launch the first annual *Berkley Hills Soap Box Derby*. We would have two days to build the vehicles and then meet on Saturday to race whatever we made. All of us ran in different directions to immediately begin the construction of our racers. *The Soap Box Derby*, by the way, is named for the old gravity-powered race carts made of planks of wood topped with wooden boxes created for the 19th century distribution of soap. Our idea, developed from the absolute necessity of lacking talent and tools, was to create a functional racer, not a fancy vehicle. It started with the primary plank that was 2"x 6" and about 5' long. The steering mechanism was a single pivot bolt fastened through the center of the plank which was connected to a 2"x4" with axles attached to support any wheels one could find. The basic building blocks to make our crude versions of the Soap Box Derby cars were everywhere. A resourceful kid could find discarded heaps of wood in most backyards, and an abandoned wagon would provide a convenient set of tires and axels. What we lacked in stability and engineering, we made up for in resourcefulness and extra nails.

The back axle was usually one piece of steel that was nailed across the six inches of wood directly behind the driver. Most drivers were smart enough to put this back axle under the main 2"x 6" primary support. One driver, however, decided to put the axle on top of the 2"x 6", and only later, after it came apart and took the seat with it, did he realize the folly of his plan.

We quickly learned that engineering was critically essential but severely lacking entirely in our endeavors. The front axles were often placed at slightly different angles, causing the tires to work against each other and resulting in slowing the vehicle or making it entirely unstable when it was being steered.

The pivot bolt for the steering mechanism had no blocking on it, so if the driver turned too far, the 2" x 4" front guidance system could suddenly jackknife, causing one's foot to be crushed in the process. The braking system was a large stick with a nail through its middle which the driver could pivot and scrape along the ground. However, it did not affect the speed of the vehicle whatsoever. One stick made from a pine tree branch broke in half the first time it was used. Another excited driver pivoted his brake the wrong way, pole vaulting his car enough that it caused his vehicle into a most spectacular wreck.

Every driver needed a means to return the cart back to the top of the hill. This effort was accomplished by utilizing a spare clothesline tied on each end of the 2x4 near the wheels. This rope served a double purpose by helping to provide some stability for steering the cart, but in most cases, the line was too short, and the cart would bang the back of the driver's heels with every step as he pulled the cart back to the starting poin

Helmets were optional. I wore a leather football helmet while one friend wore a white plastic helmet that looked fabulous but had no webbing or padding and offered no protection. Some wore no helmet; they were brave indeed. One put a red tee-shirt over his head for safety, I guess, or perhaps to make a fashion statement.

We all agreed on the rules of the race, making the "heat" races were two cars at a time. The finale would have all the cars racing simultaneously with the winner of the heats located in the front. The starting line was a crooked crack in the asphalt across Columbia Street located right at our driveway. The driveway served as a perfect pit stop so the driver could make any last-minute adjustments. The heats could also be planned with two cars aligning in our gravel driveway before being pushed out onto the street.

Word got out about our derby beyond our neighborhood, and the first weekend of races had a significant crowd of about 15 kids. Every kid, whether racing or not, had his favorite car and racer, and as the races got underway, the epic scale of the unfolding disaster was becoming apparent. The first race saw Dave's front right wheel fly off, cartwheeling him across ten feet of asphalt before he ended up in a gutter. Of course, we all ran to his aid, and when we examined his vehicle, it didn't take long before we realized that he had not used cotter pins in the holes at the end of the axle. He just used nails and hadn't bent them enough to stabilize the wheels. We would have given him a hard time for such an oversight if he hadn't been blinking back tears from his pain and embarrassment.

The second heat was equally disastrous. Wayne's vehicle was pulling hard to the left, and he overcompensated by steering extra hard to the right, crashing directly into Billy's crate. Billy lost control, both vehicles were damaged, and their owners were pretty upset by the wreck although they didn't lose much blood from their scrapes and wounds.

Finally, it was my turn to race against Tom. He had been the most creative of the drivers in getting parts for his vehicle. Tom even secretly borrowed the wheels from his dad's lawnmower. While we all admired Tom's ingenuity, he needed to get those wheels back on the lawnmower before his father got home. Now, I knew that Tom's wheels were smaller than mine, which had come off an old wagon, but his wheels were new, and mine were so old that the rubber was dry rotting, plus my axles were rusty despite the wire brushing and liberal amounts of motor oil I dribbled on them. However, I just felt in my heart that I would beat Tom, so I started the race full of optimism because I had the better side of Columbia Street, and he would have to navigate around two potholes and a section of loose asphalt.

When the starter said go, Tom's cart was immediately ahead. I yelled that he was cheating, but all the spectators and

I knew better. As his vehicle inched ahead, I pumped my weight forward and backward, trying to encourage my cart to a faster speed. Unfortunately, as I started catching up, Tom swerved to avoid the pothole. My front left tire hit his back right wheel, and both carts careened out of control. Mine went right onto the grass, and Tom did the first donut that I have ever witnessed. Nobody was hurt in our collision, but we had a bigger problem. The lawnmower wheel that had the encounter with my wheel had cracked and was beyond repair.

This trauma stopped the race as all further effort was made to save Tom's ass from being tanned by his dad when he discovered that his son had ruined the lawnmower. Nonetheless, one of the great fallbacks for kids is to deny any involvement completely, and we all agreed that was the best course of action. Tom carefully replaced the lawnmower tires and discreetly located the broken wheel on the back so it wouldn't be noticed immediately by his dad. He meticulously returned the lawnmower to its usual storage place in the garage and thought that nobody would be the wiser.

Despite everything Tom did, his dad was no dummy, and when he got home from work that evening, the first thing he noticed was a cart racer without wheels. When he inquired as to the whereabouts of the wheels his son had used on his cart, Tom broke down and confessed. The next day, Tom's dad went to the hardware store where he bought four new wheels with ball bearings(!) along with a tube of real grease. Most of the wheels on carts had sleeve bearings which were much less efficient than ball bearings. This would be a game changer for our cart racing and was a definite escalation of the sport. His dad also purchased one new wheel for his lawnmower, the cost of which would come out of Tom's meager allowance.

The inaugural Berkley Hills Soap Box Derby had been an enormous success by any measure. The crowd certainly got its fill of entertainment, although nobody crossed the finish line. Since I had reached the furthest down the hill, I declared myself the winner (pending all the drivers' protests). There were no hospital visits required, though Dave could have used a few stitches, and we learned a lot about engineering!

The first television in Berkley Hills necessitated installing the first TV antenna, which involved the whole family. My assignment was to let them know when the picture looked best.

The Parachutist

We were the first family in our neighborhood to get a television that received one channel that you could watch and a second one distorted by ghosts. The neighborhood kids all gathered at our home on Saturday mornings to watch the shows that tended to be wholesome and filled with lessons about life. *Sky King* was one such show that captured the imagination of Sam, one of our younger friends. One episode had someone parachuting out of an airplane, so young Sammy was inspired to make a parachute out of an umbrella. He lived on the second floor of a two-story house which had a balcony in the back.

One Saturday when the last show had ended, our gang was heading out to our backyard when we heard young Sammy yell from the balcony of his house, "Hey guys, look at me!" He was standing on the handrail of his balcony holding an umbrella with one hand. Without any fanfare, Sam jumped off the railing. His open umbrella immediately folded inside out. I'll never forget the sickening splat as Sam hit the cement driveway. He didn't move. I thought he was dead and so did all my friends. We just stood there in stunned silence, mouths agape. A couple of the kids went running to their respective homes, which was the only sensible thing to do when something terrible happened. Sammy's mom came out of the house screaming incoherently and accusatorily something along the lines of, "Did you put him up to this, Jimmy Gregory?" She scooped him up and put him in the car while his father got behind the wheel and raced him to the hospital. Amazingly, he was back home after only three nights at the hospital. He only suffered a compound broken leg, a concussion, and the humiliation of a new nickname, "Sky Dummy!"

Neighborhood Clans and Feuds

If you feuded with a neighbor, you needed to remember that there were tribes of relatives living on Berkley Hills, so, feuding with the one meant you were feuding with them all. There were multiple families: Gilberts, Charbaghs, Herdsmens, Bolhas, Steinbrings, Beamers, Bridges, and Kellys. There were also the Gindlespergers and Beams, but since they had mostly girls, they did not count. Once, when my brother Wayne was chased home by some of the Gilberts, our older sister Doris came to Wayne's rescue and chased them back to their home. Long lasting feuds could be started by such incidents.

Our generation of the Gregory Clan in the Westmont School District was a powerful and dominant force due to the massive production of male children. Our Gregory Clan (all first cousins), ranked from the oldest to the youngest, included Bill, Bob, Doris (the only girl), George, Warren, Donny, Dick, Bruce, Wayne, David, and then the caboose, Jimmy.

Our cousins grew up only a few blocks away from where we lived on Columbia Street, and I was the very last member of that generation, which had its positives and its negatives. The Gregory Clan had a reputation of being tough and not likely to take any crap from anyone. By the time I came along, my teachers and neighbors had affirmed attitudes toward the Gregorys. For example, my brother Dick

41

remembers sitting in detention with a half dozen or so of other kids from various grades, and four of them, George, Warren, Don, and Dick, were Gregorys.

The Gregory cousins: Don, Bob, George, Bill, and Warren

I found it sometimes confusing that I grew up not being allowed to speak to specific neighbors because of never-ending feuds that basically maintained the status of a low boil like a cold war where the participants never talked to each other. The friction was sometimes over fundamental issues like our catching an adult neighbor's attempting to steal electrical outlets when our house was newly built. However, most offenses developed over minor issues like the appearance of one encroaching on a property border or the placement of a mailbox. Nothing of great importance but essential enough to cause hard feelings

On those occasions requiring a confrontation, I always placed my money on my dad. When provoked, Pop could swell to double his size, almost like a cartoon character, but, unlike an enlarged cartoon character, you didn't want to mess with him. Neither did our neighbors.

One confrontation almost came to blows between my dad and Mr. K., who had a distinct height advantage. While the discussion was heated enough that someone called the police, my father maneuvered to the high ground on Columbia Street, negating Mr. K's height advantage. When Officer Rankin arrived on the scene, Rankin was yelling, "Don't hit him!"

Another incident that made it into family legend took place when Mrs. K was out in her garden pruning onions. When a ball accidentally landed in her yard, both my brother Wayne and Mrs. K also ran after it, and somehow, Wayne claimed that she was chasing him with a knife! After that, we were encouraged to play ball with old tin cans, and if the "ball" should go into their yard, it was OK to leave it there.

Luckily, none of our feuding neighbors had kids who were my age. So, there it stood. I never spoke to several neighbors in the 20 years I called Columbia Street my home.

Boxing Gloves

We owned two sets of boxing gloves, but I don't remember their being utilized by anyone other than as a prop in family photos.

Jimmy wearing the family boxing gloves. The victory pose was a bit premature.

The boxing gloves were always hanging in the garage in the same location, and they intrigued my friends who often mentioned boxing as a potentially fun activity. Without asking for permission, which would have caused unnecessary questions, I borrowed the gloves one day to take them over to

Randy's basement, the venue for an official neighborhood boxing match. Someone had brought a stopwatch so we could time the rounds just like the Friday night fights TV show *The Gillette Cavalcade of Sports*. We would have three one-minute sessions with 30 seconds between them, and anyone could last four minutes, even if it were a slugfest.

Randy found a galvanized washtub for the bell and a small aluminum mallet for the ringer. When the mallet hit the tub, it made a loud enough noise that it would command everyone's attention at the end of around. One of the neighboring twins had a stopwatch from Cub Scouts to time the rounds; unfortunately, he was somewhat inattentive, so the rounds could go long anywhere from 10 to 30 seconds, which seemed like an eternity when you were boxing.

The draw for the first match was between the neighbor twins, and it turned out to be very disappointing since it was more like shadow boxing. While disheartened by the lack of contact, everyone had the understanding that the twins had to live with each other, so they were not going to have it out in a public forum.

I was in the next draw, and my opponent was Randy, our host. Randy was a skinny, creepy-looking kid with dark circles around his eyes from all his allergies. To his credit, when Randy wore boxing gloves, he defended himself beyond all expectations. We also had Bernie, a neighbor who fancied himself to be a sports radio announcer. So, when he narrated the fight, he barked, "In the near corner, we have Jimmy who is looking particularly tough today as he did his push-up before entering the boxing ring. In the opposite corner is Randy, who looks wiry but is as ready as he'll ever be for this morning's match." Ding! Bernie continued with his narrative, "The fight begins, the two boxers approach each other cautiously, Jim throws a jab, then another..." That was the last thing I heard as Randy threw a roundhouse punch that landed squarely on the side of my head. If we were in a professional boxing match, it would be called a Technical Knock Out (TKO), but as we were in the privacy of Randy's basement, the fight went on. Unfortunately, Randy didn't follow with his advantage, and despite being dazed, I somehow sustained myself until the end of the first round.

When I sat down between rounds on the little stool in my corner, my head was spinning, and every nerve cell in my shaking body was demanding for me to quit. My best friend Wayne, who was talking to me in my corner, said, "You can't let RANDY beat you. If he does, you will never live it down." It was the ultimate warning from a true friend that I would lose my stature forever if I suffered a defeat. That was all I needed because when the bell rang, I jumped out at Randy like a buzz saw. I hit him, kicked him, and I would have bitten him if I could have gotten close enough. Once again, I started hearing Bernie's announcements, "Just when we thought Jimmy was ready to throw in the towel, he has come out of his corner like a wounded lion. He is using a boxing style that is somewhat unorthodox but effective." So, the first round went to Randy, the second round went to me, which meant the third and final round would decide the match. We had only boxed two minutes in total, but our arms and legs were wobbly. Never in the history of humankind had two minutes seemed to consume hours of excruciating effort. Neither of us could launch any offense in the third round which meant the judges (everyone in attendance) got to vote on who won the match. Since I had the most friends, I won the split-decision. Randy's brother Andy voted for him, and I was happy with this hard-earned but improbable victory. The life lesson I learned is never to take an opponent for granted.

My Best Friend

Wayne Miller was my first friend and no doubt my best friend. He has been mentioned several times already in these stories, but I feel that he deserves a special section.

Wayne on the right zipping up! The neighbor Beamer twins and me on the left. In our back yard on the Merry-Go-Round that my dad built.

I don't have any recollection of the first time I met Wayne; we were just always friends and did everything together as kids. We experienced many simple but rewarding adventures like sleeping in the summer on my family's back porch and camping in a tent in the backyard. As we grew older, the camping adventures became ever more daring. We would raid the neighborhood apple and pear trees, eating the fruit until we got sick; what fun.

When we were about eight years old, we joined a local organization of Marine Cadets that would meet at the old Berkley Hills Grade School. We would go to the meetings to learn marksmanship, to learn how to march, and to learn how to conduct different drills. Our uniform was a white tee-shirt and white plastic helmet. After the meeting, we would run as fast as we could to my home to watch the TV show about WWII submarines, *Sea Hunt.* As we ran the two blocks home, we would yell the sound a sub makes before diving, "Oooogaaa, ooooogaaaa." I can't imagine what the neighbors thought as we raced past bellowing those sounds.

A newspaper clipping about the Marine Cadets.

Sledding Down Berkley Road

Everybody knew you NEVER went sledding down Berkley Road after a fresh snow because it was just too steep. Hell, there were a lot of roads to use for sledding without attempting Berkley Road. After all, the area was called Berkley *Hills*. In Pennsylvania, all power was generated by coal, which provided a huge amount of waste called *ashes*. In those days, ashes were used instead of salt to help drivers navigate the snow-covered roads. It was only common sense that you would only try Berkley Road after it had been thickly "ashed." Then sparks would fly off the runners of the sled, and even then, you still went out of control from the incredible steepness of the road.

Why would anyone try to challenge Berkley Road? Well, becoming an instant legend is the only reason. Take our friend Bob Bridges who built a homemade wheeled cart constructed explicitly for such a purpose. The cart consisted of a giant metal mailbox with a hole cut in the top for his head. Bob lost a wheel on his attempt of Berkley Road and flipped end-over-end five or six times. Luckily, he remembered to pull in his head before he was decapitated, but he got pummeled and finished with both eyes black and his head swollen like a lopsided melon. What a living legend!

Wayne Miller and I were determined to attempt one of the most death-defying feats of our young lives by sledding down Berkley Road before it was ashed. To be sure we were giving it the complete effort, we started with the run-up the alley, adding at least a couple of hundred feet BEFORE we veered down Berkley Road. To be sure there were no cars coming, we had a spotter at the corner of the Warren Street and Berkley Road intersection. We decided that the double-deck formation was the best way to travel with Wayne on the bottom to oversee the steering. I was on top and responsible for the navigation, breaking, ballast, and co-piloting. In other words, I would just be hanging on for my dear life. The conditions that day were perfect. It had recently snowed on top of another hard-packed snow, and Berkley Road had not yet been ashed.

As the run started, we were confident that we would break the sound barrier that day, and we darn near accomplished it. We were immediately flying, and it was amazing that we negotiated the slight dogleg turn from the alley to Berkley Road. I remember our spotter yelling for us to slow down right before we hit the steep part. Of course, we didn't need his advice because we already knew we were utterly out-of-control. My recollection at this point has grown hazy. We crashed into a tree somewhere around three-quarters down Berkley Road. I do remember Wayne yelling, "Bail-out, bail-out!" The effect was spectacular, and I don't know how much further we went sans-sled. Wayne and I had numerous scratches and bruises, but the collision with the tree utterly destroyed the sled, and only thing that concerned us was telling his parents that we demolished the sled. Ouch.

Not having learned our lesson on Berkley Road, we took our bikes down Sell Street that summer – a continuous slope of about a mile from top to bottom. I don't know how fast we were going, but it was so rapid that the bikes quivered from the speed. We completely burned out our coaster brakes, literally smoking when we got to the bottom; thank goodness they worked. However, when we finally came to a stop, the brakes immediately froze and completely locked-up the wheels so we could no longer ride the bikes at all. We walked the bikes all the way home with the rear tires immobilized.

Another close call came in a car. Wayne's dad Earl owned a Corvair, and one day, when we were about eleven years old, Wayne announced that he knew how to drive that car. I scoffed as eleven-year-olds tend to do. To prove it to me, we got into the car, and when he released the brake and put the car in neutral, it started to coast down their driveway across the street in front of their house toward a significant cliff that didn't have guardrails. Luckily, Earl saw the vehicle moving and jumped in and stopped it. I had never heard Earl curse before.

Wayne was like a member of our family. He attended all our family picnics in our backyard, whether invited or not. My mom would always set a place for him, just assuming he would be there. One day, we happened to be playing at Wayne's house when his mom asked me if I would like to stay for dinner. Thinking about how many times Wayne had eaten at our home, I thought it was a good idea to accept the invitation. I should have called my mom to see if it was OK to eat at Wayne's house, but the thought never occurred that Thanksgiving was a special family dinner. When I got home and told my mom that I wasn't hungry – well, let's just say it was the only time she raised a hand to me. Lesson learned.

My brother Dick, my wife Evelyn, and I visited Wayne one last time before he passed from ALS.

The Snow Tunnel

My hometown is in the snowbelt, and snow falls of 10-12" are standard weekly entertainment from December until March. So, with so much snow, you need to do things for recreation. Of course, there were obligatory snowball fights. Yes, there were snow forts built of every size and complexity, but one of the more inventive sports was the snow igloo. Snow from shoveled walks or driveways would be piled quite high, maybe six feet or more, as packed snowbanks, and that is when a snow igloo could be fashioned by intrepid kids. Some of the igloos were big enough inside to hold several kids at once.

My friend Wayne and I decided to craft a snow tunnel one March after a late-season snowstorm and the subsequent plowing along the street in front of Wayne's house set up the perfect snow embankment for the endeavor. I told my dad what we had planned and my need to borrow a few tools for the project. He didn't object, but he decided to accompany me to where we undertook the task. Wayne started on one side of the embankment, and I started on the other. We worked hard until we made a small hole between us and could see each other. At the moment we touched hands through the hole, the entire tunnel collapsed on us. I couldn't move, nor could I scream. I was suffocating with the air squeezed right out of me. I was dying and couldn't do a thing about it. Suddenly, I felt strong hands around my legs, and my dad pulled me out of the tunnel. Wayne's dad did the same for him. I can't imagine what instinct my dad sensed to go with me on this exploration because he didn't usually provide such oversite. I can't imagine why he and Wayne's dad decided to standby and talk while we were digging. I do know unequivocally that my dad's instinct saved both of our lives.

Pop's Schedule

We always needed to be aware of Dad's work shift because if he worked 11:00 pm-7:00 am (night turn), he would be sleeping in the daytime, and we needed to be somewhat more quiet than usual (which was never). Unfortunately, it seemed when Pop worked night turn, things happened that would wake anyone from a sound sleep.

Pop worked in the 9"2 Gautier Mill as a heater.

One time Dick and Doris were alone downstairs while Pop, who had worked night turn, was sleeping upstairs. It was early afternoon, and they decided to close the French doors to the kitchen and pretend to be entertaining by making some cocktails in fancy glasses that Doris brought down from the cabinets. There is no recollection of what they were drinking, but they were having a hell of a good time laughing while still trying to be quiet. Then they heard the dreaded sound of Pop getting out of bed, and they both stared at each other petrified. They were caught!

Burn Down the House or Wake Up Pop?

Bruce and Wayne made a narrow escape from waking Pop and from burning down the house when they made a batch of rocket fuel that accidentally caught fire. Testing rock fuel was a continual process since we knew wooden matchheads were not enough to blast our rockets into the air, and the *laboratory* we used was what we called the "playroom" adjoining Bruce and Wayne's bedroom. When the twins made two-quart bottles of the new fuel, one tiny spark set them on fire.

Shown here is the twins' bedroom with the "playroom" to the right. Note the chemistry set to the far right.

Pop, having worked night turn, was sleeping in the upper bedroom, so Bruce and Wayne closed the door to their bedroom, put towels under the door so the smoke wouldn't go up to his room, and then opened the windows and fanned the smoke outside. There was so much smoke that they thought the neighbors would call the fire department. The flames were fierce but were put out quickly. They had scorched the slanted ceiling of the playroom and left two black circles. Mom, fortunately, helped paint the scorched ceiling, and the twins don't think Pop ever knew. I wouldn't bet on that.

Rockets

While we are on the subject, we might as well discuss our obsession with rockets. This was the dawn of the space age with Sputnik 1 launching in 1957. We were glued to the TV news with every advancement or set back the USA had against its archrival the Soviet Union. From my earliest memories, the Gregory boys were thinking about rockets.

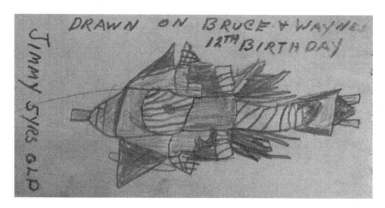

Even a novice will be able to identify this as a multi-stage, liquid fuel rocket (circa 1954).

There were three primary issues concerning the building and launching of a rocket. First, what is the fuel? Second, what kind of vehicle is appropriate? Third, which is arguably the most important, how do you launch the rocket without getting blown up in the process? All three issues brought their share of successes and failures.

The most readily available fuel was the kitchen match. The match heads from wooden matches were cut and packed in an appropriate vehicle. I remember a good-looking rocket made from a tin can that my three brothers had filled with match heads. The launchpad was the heavy iron base of a floor lamp, and there was a loop of wire around the rocket and lamp pole to guide the missile as it took off. This was an excellent preparation for the launch, and my brothers went over to Berkley Hills golf course and found the perfect sand trap for the night launch. Using a garbage can lid as a shield, Dick lit the rocket. It was impressive and roared for a minute or two but never actually gained lift-off. When the smoke cleared, it glowed red for quite a while. Upon close examination, the rocket had welded itself onto the iron base pad and had also blown an impressive trench into the sand trap.

When I was old enough to play with matches, I began my own series of attempted rocket launches. I experimented with rolled-up aluminum foil but quickly learned that because it couldn't hold up to the heat that the rocket generated, it would rupture the side of the rocket. The most effective rockets were made from those small cardboard tubes that come with clothes hangers from the laundry. I would fill them with rocket fuel carefully concocted of match heads and black powder because too much black powder simply created a bomb. I don't remember when we got that little red can of black powder at our house, but I do remember thinking it would potentially make good rocket fuel. Anyway, I launched the fueled rocket in our backyard with a fuse made of tightly rolled newspaper. I would also shoot the missiles through discarded cardboard tubes from old Christmas wrapping paper. Since the rockets had no fins, they were highly erratic, and they could potentially rebound at you. So, the launch control center needed to be behind the sandbox with a protective shield in front. I probably had six successful launches, as defined by getting off the launch pad, and six complete failures during my career as a junior rocketeer.

Squibs

In terms of danger, squibs were a close cousin to rockets because they are used in the coal mines to blow up dynamite. The miners would drill a hole in the mine face, fill it with dynamite, then place the squibs into the dynamite, and then ignite them. Boom! Down would fall the coal!
Dick was our squib man. He had somehow found a stash of squibs that Pop had brought home and thought he had effectively hidden. The squibs, when lit, were like 4th of July sparklers. The playground at Berkley School was a place to discharge these marvels, sometimes several in quick succession, sometimes toward each other. Bruce and Wayne mainly watched. It was Dick's show.

The boxes looked a little bit like a narrower box of wooden matches, and there must have been a dozen or more boxes, each like a tiny straw with a pigtail fuse. When lit, the fuse would burn down to the black powder and quickly burn for a few seconds. If you put them in a pipe or tube of some kind, you could direct them to the opposing team. Otherwise, they just went crazy in any direction.

It was the Fourth of July, and Dick had found that some mice had eaten into the boxes of squibs. So, he spent about an hour draining the ones that the mice had damaged and used the little box that they came in to collect the powder. He had accumulated about 1/16 of the box with the black powder piled up at one end and took it over to the Berkley School. Unfortunately, no one was there, so he sat down on the front steps. Now, what should he do? Dick lit the other end of the box and watched as it burned. A few grains had shifted out of place, and as he attempted to brush them back with his finger. That's when the box went, "Woosh", and burned off his eyebrows. He grabbed his left hand with his right and thought, "That was a close call!" Then he looked at his left hand, and that's when he noticed the skin on his knuckles had slid over. Then his hand started to drip clear fluid. Dick went home, and as Mom let him in the back door, he held his hand behind his back and said, "Now Mom, don't get excited." The Johnstown newspaper *The Tribune-Democrat* stated in a short article, "There was just one 4th of July injury this year."

Mom's Cooking

We had a gas stove that required using a white lever to turn on the gas. It was then lit with a match. One time, Mom made homemade vegetable soup, and it must have been delicious because Dick was slurping it up and saying how good it was. Mom said that's because she'd put everything in it. Just then, Dick said, "You sure did!" as he pulled a half-burnt match out of his bowl. Poor Mom couldn't believe that when she had placed the spoon down on the match to keep the counter clean, the match stuck to the spoon and found its way into the soup.

Snowballing cars

Throwing snowballs at cars was a major league sport on Berkley Hills. There was the danger element of scaring the hell out of the driver of the ambushed vehicle, but there was also the danger of being caught, so we usually chose high ground for setting the ambush. The top of Goucher Street was such a good location - information passed on from brother to brother. There was also the skill aspect because when throwing snowballs at cars, you had to "lead" the cars just right to hit them. It was an acquired skill.

Getting caught was not something that concerned us too much; unfortunately, my brothers Bruce and Wayne, who were

about 12 years old at the time, and their good friend Bob
Bridges hit the wrong car. After pummeling several vehicles,
they turned around, and there were 4 or 5 teenage kids behind
them. My brother Bruce and Bob immediately jumped over a
wall and down the hill toward and across Goucher Street and
scattered with the teens in hot pursuit. Bruce hid under a pine
tree on Claycomb's farm, and Bob circled, eventually arriving
back at his home. Nobody knew what happened to Wayne.
Bruce eventually returned home, hoping to find Wayne there
but with no luck. Bruce didn't mention anything to Mom or
Dad who were curious why the brothers were not together?
Bruce acted nonchalantly and just watched television with the
folks until a half-frozen Wayne returned home at around 10:00
p.m. that night.

Wayne apparently ran the wrong way toward the teens
and was caught immediately. They drove him to an abandoned
restaurant called *Picken Chicken* located on an isolated
highway, and they let him out of the car. He was forced to walk
6.5 miles back home along a dark, dangerous, remote road on a
winter's night! He was so lucky not to have been killed. Years
later, one of our cousins died on that very same highway in a
car wreck.

Tree Houses

Our neighbor, Earl Buchan, and my brother Dick were playing Indians and had a cozy little fire in the center of their teepee, which was a hollowed out dying tree with an inverted "V" entrance. Since it was hollow up through a branch that had broken off, the tree had a natural chimney. At the moment when the fire was burning inside the teepee, Mom and Pop called for Dick to come up from the woods and go with us while we went to the A&P by the Roxy Theater so that he would stay out of trouble.

On our way home from the store, a fire engine with sirens wailing was a short distance behind our car and seemed to be going in the same direction. When Dad let it pass, it turned right down to Columbia Street and into the back alley to get as close to that hollow tree as possible. Dad went down to help fight the blaze as Dick sneaked up to our attic window to watch. The flames were spewing into the air like a blowtorch from the draft up the hollow tree.

At another time, Bruce, Wayne, and a neighbor, Barry Weigel, built a vast 8'x 8' electrified treehouse on nearby Derby Street. They crafted the treehouse high up around the main shaft of a large tree. Coincidentally, a guy who lived on Derby Street who worked on alarm systems tossed away many dry cell batteries when they were too weak to use for the alarms.

The "three treehouse craftsmen" recovered a whole assortment of these batteries and by wiring them in a series, captured enough juice to illuminate a small light. When Dick went to see the treehouse, he climbed up above it and bounced on the roof to scare those who were inside. Dick looked in and was amazed that they had electric light inside. He was probably equally surprised at the significant collection of *Playboy* magazines that his younger brothers had amassed.

Bob Bridges and Wayne once built a dugout hut in the trees between Bob's house and the Berkley Hills cemetery. It was half of a hole in the ground and half of an above-ground shelter. They rigged up a telephone to Bob's house, and their first call was Bob's Mom saying that our mom had called, and it was time for Wayne to go home for dinner. Highly technical for those days.

My tree houses were low to the ground and unspectacular, but I must have felt like I missed something because on my 40th birthday, I built a significant treehouse in my backyard, "for my kids." It had secret trap doors and a balcony and satisfied my long-repressed desire to create a treehouse of my own.

The Woods

The woods behind our house were a paradise that held countless mysteries and adventures. There was a dump where a multitude of glass bottles flashed invitations to be broken by anyone owning a BB gun, and there were plenty of places to build tree houses. A spring seeped out of the hillside and formed a small pond that was big enough to house lizards and snakes. There was also an inexplicable set of cement steps in the middle of the woods. I used to imagine they were built there as the entrance to a mysterious magical world.

An old railroader's watch found in the woods behind our home.

I didn't know it at the time, but the steps gave me a lifelong interest in archaeology. How did they get there? Who used them? Why? It turned out that the steps were built during the Great Depression in the 1930s by the Civilian Conservation Corps (CCC) as part of the Roxbury Park project.

Once, while walking my dog through the woods, my dog started to dig at something in the ground, and we discovered an old railroader's watch. It was in perfect condition, even though it had been buried for a long time. The only thing showing was the round crystal of the face, but at first, I couldn't see anything else. I've always been curious about the heritage and previous ownership of the watch. There must be a fascinating story associated with the treasure. I have had experts in antique watches evaluate the prize, and while it isn't worth a lot, it is priceless to me.

The mysterious steps in the woods. There are two types of plants shown in this photo. One you could pull up by the stem and it would come out with a ball of dirt on the roots. They made great bombs you could toss at someone, and a hit would douse them with dirt. The other type of plant was called "cow itch" and would give you a very itchy rash. The two plants looked very similar, so you had to be careful of what plant you were grabbing to bomb someone.

Strange Sounds

Sometimes our house made strange sounds. One time, when Doris and Dick came home from school and were alone in the kitchen waiting for mom and dad to arrive home from the store, they heard a God-awful sound. They both gave each other a perplexed look and when they heard it again, they realized that it was coming from upstairs. Both armed themselves with butcher knives and began to explore, Doris pushing Dick ahead of her. The death moan was coming from the bedroom at the first landing, and they entered the bedroom with the knives raised at the ready. When they eased over to the window and looked across to the Kelly's house, they discovered the source of the moans. Our neighbor, Ron Kelly had been given a school tuba and was sitting in his bedroom was squeezing out a sound as best he could. Mystery solved!

Another occurrence of a strange sound happened when I was home from school because I had a slight fever, and after school was over, I was jealous that I couldn't be in the backyard playing basketball with my brothers and their friends. Suddenly, I heard a noise in the attic that sounded like steps. I was petrified. My mom was at the store, but just then, my dad walked in the house from work. I breathlessly told him there was someone in the attic. He, too, could hear the same noise, and we carefully approached the attic steps just as the intruder was coming down the steps. My dad drew back, ready to punch the robber right in the kisser. That's when my brother Wayne, carrying a stack of comic books, was luckily identified just before Pop was ready to bash out his lights. Sorry brother, you should've told me you were in the house!

Be Careful, My Dog Bites!

The first dog I remember in our family was a border collie. I recall "Sparky" jumping up and knocking me down when I was very young, but Sparky turned out to be a great dog. When Mom and Dad would tie a note on her and release her to find Dick. Sparky would diligently discover that he was playing football in one of several places: in the cemetery, in Roxbury Park, at Berkley Hill Golf Course, etc. The note would usually say, "Dick, come home for supper." Unfortunately, while Dick was away in the service, sweet Sparky was killed accidentally by Tony, the vegetable man who came around to our neighborhood with his truck filled with produce. While he was stopped out in front of our home, Sparky lay down under the truck to get some shade, I guess.

As my older siblings grew up and away from home, I was more and more on my own. My folks decided that I needed to have a companion, and what could be better than a dog for a young boy? The breed they choose was dachshund (aka *wiener dog* and *dog from hell*). His full name was Herr Hannibal von Jamie, but we called him "Hans." I loved the dog, but it was loyal and protective to the point of being a significant nuisance. It was also fearless and vicious against any threat, and we had multiple warnings about the seriousness of Hans as a public danger. One time this dog was barking through the front door at the milkman and then ran through the house, bounced against the back screened door, wedged it open enough to get out, and ran around the house to attack the milkman. We heard glass breaking as the milkman was throwing bottles of milk to protect himself from the dog. There was just no compromising with Hans. He reacted viciously towards anyone outside the immediate family, and in hindsight, he should have permanently visited the farm before anyone got hurt.

My friend, Wayne, however, was generally tolerated by Hans because Wayne always greeted him cheerfully, and even after barking a warning, Hans would allow Wayne to pass without any further scrutiny. One morning Wayne brought a large soup bone for Hans. What a wonderful treat for the dog! As Wayne put the bone in the dog's food bowl, Hans, without warning, jumped up and bit Wayne right on the nose. There was a huge amount of blood, and we had no idea how much damage Wayne's nose had received. Pop jumped up and immediately threw Hans down the steps into the basement. My mom found a seat for Wayne as he was beginning to become pale and faint. Pop called Mr. Miller, telling him that our dog had bitten Wayne and that his son needed to go to the hospital. Mr. Miller, not realizing the seriousness of the situation, joked, "Even the dog doesn't like him." It was a terrible situation and one of the worst days of my young life. At the hospital, nothing could be done to help. Plastic surgeons stitched the wound, but in those days, reconstructive surgery was in its infancy and was not a consideration. Unfortunately, Wayne carried the scars of that day for the rest of his life.

As for Hans, it marked the closing chapter for my dog. He wasn't sent to the farm but exiled from our family's embrace. His home was now the basement, and he would hide behind the furnace if anyone came down the stairs. I would sit on the bottom step and wait for Hans to come over for hugs and a chat. We were still buddies, but we both knew there was no going back to the previous carefree life.

It was standard procedure for my dad to let the dog out for a quick pee before bed. One time the dog didn't come back, and early the following morning, we got a call from our neighbors saying that our dog was on their porch and appeared to be sick. I immediately went to their house and found Hans covered in an old blanket. He looked up at me, wagged his tail a little, and then died in my arms as I carried him home. We didn't know if he had been poisoned, had been hit by a car, or died of hypothermia. In any event, he was gone, and I was probably the only one in mourning. Pop took me to the movies that day, and since it was the only time he took me to the cinema, I assume it was to take my mind off the terrible series of events that lead to Han's demise. I remember silently crying through the movie.

Hans, the dog that terrorized everyone but me.

Sunbeams & Rainbows

A brand-new church had been built a few miles from our house, and the staff was promoting Summer Bible School to kids of elementary school age. It must have been relatively inexpensive to sign-up because everyone in our neighborhood was in attendance. They divided the group into "Sunbeams" and "Rainbows," and we competed in little contests such as who could sing a particular song the best, who could put on the best play, or who could draw the best picture of baby Jesus, etc. Everything was a friendly competition, but where it got interesting was when they competed for donations. As I recall, there was a big scale in the front of the recreation room where penny donations were received on either the Rainbow or Sunbeam side of the scales. Well, it didn't take long for kids to bring in rolls of pennies, and the money from these penny donations added up!

Graduation from Summer Bible School

It was at the Summer Bible School where I met my first black friend. I had never thought about different races, and it just never occurred to me that one race was different from another. World War II had been over for less than a decade, but there were still residual attitudes against "Dirty Krauts!" when we played army in our backyard.

Nevertheless, we never associated this term with any anger or meanness toward our neighbor, who was of German descent. It might have been an entirely different perception from our German friend Alex when he played army with us.

We just never discussed or even thought about it. He might have, but we didn't. Race issues were a topic that didn't cross our minds.

I had never before encountered a black fellow my age, and when the teacher who introduced us said we should shake hands, we did. I instinctively looked at my hand to see if any of his color had rubbed off on my hand, and I remember how ashamed I felt for having done that. Anyway, Willie and I immediately went off together, and he became my friend for that day and for the remainder of Summer Bible School. I later told my dad about my initial actions with Willie, and he said, "We are all the same under the skin." That became my governing philosophy thereafter, and I still believe it works today.

Taking Out Ashes

We all had our chores, and mine was to feed and take care of the rabbits. My twin brothers had the job of taking out the ashes from our coal-fired furnace in the basement. It was a dirty job requiring some skill to minimize the dust from the ashes. The ashes were shoveled out from the furnace's lower door and slowly lowered into metal buckets that would hold about five or six shovels. Each bucket needed to be carried up the basement steps to the garage. We placed the buckets of ashes on a wagon or on a sled when the ashes needed to be taken out in the winter. The sled could hold three-buckets; the wagon only two. The ashes needed to be moved to the backyard, which was about 100 feet away, and they would be dumped onto an ash pile. Even if it were carefully done, there was a minimum amount of dirt that would always alight on your clothes.

Saturday was our day to do these chores, and the twins liked to sleep in that day, often sleeping past noon and, thus, wasting the day. At some point, I just felt it was easier for me to take out the ashes rather have a family argument about who was responsible for doing chores. I was up early on Saturdays and didn't mind the work. That work ethic stuck with me all my life, and I always found it easier to do the job sooner than wait. Schoolwork, however, was the exception to the rule.

The Gregory Games

During the Olympics, our brother Dick became inspired to create the *Gregory Games*. We each tossed a brick and measured the distance to determine the winner. We had a long jump event, and also a high jump, which utilized a slowly raised broom handle to see who could jump the most elevated level. I remember an iron bar shaped like a javelin, but it was far too heavy for me even to lift. Dick had a great imagination and often inspired us to try different things. After Dick went to see the movie "Ivanhoe," we made shields from the tops of 5-gallon roofing tar cans, painted them with our crests, and battled with wooden swords and homemade lances. We used our imaginations a lot and were never, ever bored.

The Command Tent and Dick's Radio

Dick purchased an Army surplus command tent, which he set up in the backyard. It had four windows equipped with removable plexiglass. He would sleep in this tent and tune his crystal radio set while wearing a headset and moving the cat whisker over the stone. (A crystal detector is an electronic component used in some early 20th-century radio receivers. It consists of a piece of crystalline mineral which rectifies the alternating current of a radio signal. The most common type was the so-called *cat whisker detector*, which consisted of a piece of crystalline mineral with a fine wire touching its surface.) Dick had to connect it to a solid copper rod that he pounded into the ground so the radio would work, and his plan was successful.

Here the Gregory Boys (Bruce, Jim, Wayne, and Dick) built a raft of logs on the Juniata River.

Our "Cottage"

Dad decided to purchase a lot behind a line of cottages that bordered on the Raystown Branch of the Juniata River near Everett, a borough in Bedford County, PA, where we would go to fish and swim. We called the lot *our cottage*, but it was just a small piece of land. After Dick reached the age of 23, he took his tent over to Bedford County, and after he married, the tent served as the newlyweds' (Dick and Sally) honeymoon getaway. Their bridal bed was a nice glider cushion placed on two large parallel branches covered with many smaller cross sticks. Ah well, we're all of Viking blood. During Dick and Sally's honeymoon, Old "Scrubby Graham", a distant relative who was keeping an eye out for our "cottage," called Dad to let him know that Dick was over in Bedford with a girl.

School Smarts

I knew in elementary school that there were high expectations for my academic performance. While I had a sense that I was not performing as expected in school, I didn't know why or what precisely the conferences were all about, but it became increasingly clear that I was an underperformer through grade school. If anyone had asked me, I would have told them I was bored senseless with school. Later in life, I realized that I was a slow starter and a strong finisher. However, once the stigma begins to infect the student in grade school, it isn't easy to cure.

Lester C. Hillegas was the principal of Goucher Street Elementary School. He looked a lot like Abraham Lincoln without the beard, and rumor had it that Mr. Hillegas carried an electric paddle up his sleeve that he could produce quicker than a switchblade knife.

Once, when I was in fourth grade, Mr. Hillegas visited our classroom during recess. All the other students were allowed to go outside, and while he specifically came to have a chat with me, he made it look like a casual encounter. There was small talk about my brothers, whom he had taught. I can remember his asking about my interests, and I told him I was very good at checkers; I even challenged him to a match. Much to my surprise, he accepted my challenge and quickly destroyed me in the shortest game of checkers of my young career. That visit stuck with me, and I am sure he was there to evaluate my academic ability. My conclusion was that if judged by my awful performance in checkers (what I claimed was my strength), I would indeed end up in the equivalent of elementary Siberia. I don't think I fully recovered from that evaluation until my freshman year in college, when I began to gain some self-confidence for my academic and artistic capabilities.

Eddie the Snitch and Little Johnny

My personal and social horizons were spreading even while my academic interests remained unfertilized. I recently came across my 4th-grade class picture and can still name all the students without hesitation. I got along with my fellow students in elementary school but had mixed feelings about my teachers and started to get the well-earned reputation of being a smart-ass.

Our assemblies took place in the school cafeteria. As one such group gathered, there was a lull while waiting for the principal to arrive. For reasons that I'll never understand, I started pounding on the table and chanting, "We want food! We want food!" Well, that went viral, and in about 5 seconds and the entire assembly joined in. I felt a little vulnerable since I had started it, but who would know that I was the instigator?

Mr. Hillegas walked in and put up his hands until everyone stopped chanting. He then said, "Well, I had a treat for you today, but since you misbehaved, you can all go back to your classrooms and think about your actions. I will find out who was responsible for starting this conduct." My blood ran cold. I was in serious trouble.

Mr. Hillegas stood at the exit and frowned at every student. Eddie, who was sitting at my table and was directly in front of me as we were exiting, stopped near Mr. Hillegas and said clear as a bell, "Jimmy Gregory started chanting and pounding the table." Eddie then pointed me out to Mr. Hillegas in case he didn't recognize me. It was a surreal scene. I would have shanked Eddie right then and there if I had known what shanking meant. Mr. Hillegas put his hand on the small of Eddie's back and just gave him a push to keep him walking. Mr. Hillegas then glared at me with a frown while I was looking at his sleeve to see if the electric paddle would be launched. He then gave me a slight push out the door to keep the line moving. I never heard another word except Eddie telling everyone he knew that I had started the commotion.

Interestingly, it had the opposite effect of what I expected. Instead of being seen as a social outcast, I found that I had some "bad-boy" credibility among my peers, and I liked it.

"Follow me fellow students!" I can remember every one of my 4th Grade classmates.

This little power trip ended abruptly one day when my friend, Johnny, who was the shortest person in the class, was being reseated to the front of the class so that he could better see the teacher and the chalkboard. Lord knows why I thought it would be funny to shoutout, "Little Johnny moves to the front of the class!" The teacher turned and slapped me on the side of the head so hard that I thought I heard a bell ringing as I lay sprawled across the floor. Lesson learned: Little Johnny was off-limits.

The Strike

Life at home took a whole different atmosphere when the steel company union decided to strike against the management. My dad became somber, and family spending was reduced to bare necessities. The house seemed colder because my dad didn't use as much coal in the furnace. I remember eating so much potato soup that to this day, I find it hard to eat any soup. Sometimes we tried to put some fun into the situation, and I can remember singing a song, "We eat like kings."

Photo of Pop as a heater at the steel mill. He had to determine when the steel was the right temperature to advance to the rolling mill.

My mom and dad had more arguments when the union would strike, and my only hope was to wish it was over. After the strike was over when my dad finally did go back to work, I would always say goodbye with, "Watch out for lions, tigers, and bears, and tell your boss to go jump in the lake." He would promise to do all of that!

Root Beer

We would periodically make a batch of homemade root beer. It was a whole big production, and everyone was involved in preparing all the elements. We used a large copper tub for mixing the root beer, and we carefully poured the root beer through a funnel into the bottles we had sterilized. The bottles were then sealed and transported to the basement and carefully laid on their sides on wooden shelves that doubled as beds for a Cold War bomb shelter (just in case). As the root beer fermented, the bottles would be under so much pressure that the ceramic, rubber, and wire stoppers needed to be released periodically. If we waited too long to relieve the stress, we would hear the sudden "bang" as a bottle exploded. Sometimes, one explosion would set off a chain reaction, and three or four more would blow. To relieve the pressure after one bottle had exploded was serious business. We employed helmets, goggles, heavy winter coats, and gloves to handle the bottles while each one was burped. A second collaborator would hold a tin garbage can lid like a shield to block possible glass shrapnel should one of the unburped bottles explode during the process.

Now, all of this may sound like an unnecessary danger since root beer could be purchased at any store, but the flavor of homemade root beer is unlike any other flavor in this world. It is perfectly delicious. I was too young to participate in the bottles' burping, but I was old enough to appreciate the results.

Orangeade was another concoction that my dad used to make for our Annual 4th of July holiday picnics in our backyard. Orangeade was created by utilizing the same copper tub that mixed the root beer, but this process was faster and with a lot less risk unless one drank too much. I can remember hundreds of orange slices going into the tub along with a precise amount of water and a five-pound bag of sugar. We stirred the ingredients, and then when it tasted just right, we began to use a ladle to distribute the drinks into cups with ice. Those who couldn't wait dipped their cups right into the concoction. Oh, my goodness, that was the taste of the 4th of July! I once drank so much of it that I broke out in a serious case of hives and had to be rushed to the doctor's office. Apparently, I was almost delirious, mumbling something like, "Scratch, scratch, itch, itch!"

Golf Ball Hawking at Berkley Hills Golf Course

Ball hawking is the sport of retrieving lost golf balls and selling them back to golfers who had hit them out of bounds, and there were several places at the Berkley Hills Golf Course where the hawker could find errant golf balls. The course had some holes where golfers had to hit over a wooded valley to get to the fairway, but very few golfers succeeded, and most were happy to pay 10 cents to have their ball retrieved from the woods. The hawker would watch when golfers approached the tee and then step behind a tree when the golfer struck the ball. You could tell by the "whack" of the hit whether the ball would carry the valley. If the ball started hitting the trees, you had to hope you were not hit with a ricochet while keeping an eye out for where it landed.

Several trees had been cut down, and they tended to funnel balls that might roll down the hill. You could easily find a half dozen golf balls just by walking through the valley. Each would be worth 5-10-15 cents, and a Titleist golf ball in perfect condition could bring in 25-30 cents. A good day of ball-hawking would bring in $1.25-2.00, which made me feel good.

I also learned something about the game of golf while ball-hawking. Exceptionally few golfers seemed to enjoy the sport. I would estimate that 90% of the golfers whom we could hear in our valley positions were miserable with the game. Nearly all the golfers cursed after they hit the ball, whether they made it over the valley or not. I think that is why I never had any interest in the sport. If you don't enjoy it, why play it?

My brother, Bruce is by far the best golf ball hawker I know. He worked the leaves
and branches of the valley and could find on any given occasion twice as many balls as I could. Once when we played a round of golf at my club in Connecticut, Bruce ended up with a half-dozen more balls than he started the game. He can always spot the out-of-place golf ball.

Wayne, Jimmy, and Bruce wearing our best outfits!
One of the blue spruce Christmas trees in the back yard.

The Junior Golf Tournament

Bruce was 11 years old and entered the Berkley Hills Junior Golf Tournament. He had a collection of old hickory shafted and broken clubs that had taped-on grips. His favorite club was a steel-headed 4-iron that was slightly bent where it connects to the shaft. Bruce lost his first match and was relegated to the second-tier group called the "Beaten 8". When he didn't want to play anymore, Dick said, "You can do this! AND I will caddy for you." Bruce won the next three matches and won the "Beaten 8". When the final game was tied and Bruce had to hit the ball across the valley to the #8 green, Dick told Bruce to take a deep breath with his normal swing. His shot landed within two feet, and he two-putted to win the hole. Bruce's best round was an even 100, which won him $4.00 and a plaid headcover. The pro also gave Bruce an old golf bag someone had thrown away. Bruce didn't play again until after he got out of the Navy at age 26, and it took him two more years to break 100, which is a feat that I have never achieved.

The Sunday Newspaper

My twin brothers had a newspaper route that delivered the Sunday edition of *The Pittsburgh Press*. This job was modest as these entrepreneurial businesses go, but it gave them responsibility and some pocket money for their efforts. It was an excellent taste of capitalism, and I enjoyed being a small part of the action. After delivering the prepaid newspapers to subscribers, money had to be collected from those who had requested the paper but had not yet paid. My job was to collect from the difficult clientele because it was thought that nobody would be mean to a kid. At least that was the theory. I vividly remember my brothers sending me into Nipper's house to collect the 35 cents that he put on the bedstand beside his bed where he would be sleeping. Nipper was my oldest brother's age, so he was old enough to rent his one-room apartment in the back of someone's house. Bruce and Wayne asked me to go down the alley and into his house to collect the money and drop off the paper. Most of the time, this worked out well, but there were times when Nipper was dead drunk and had forgotten to put the money out, so I had to rouse him. There were other times when he would have a girl who had stayed overnight, and she would find it strange and somewhat amusing that a young boy had walked into the bedroom looking for money.

We always had a wagon full of extra papers that we would sell at the old Berkley School that had been converted into a church. As the service let out, I would stand out yelling, "Get your *Pittsburgh Press* Sunday edition, only 35 cents." My brothers had coin changers on their belts, and the church business was fast and furious for twenty minutes. Any papers we didn't sell would be returned to the distributor.

One Sunday paper would be set aside for our own enjoyment!

Gathering Scrap

Scrap metal was a valuable commodity. We lived in a steel town, so even as kids, we were aware of scrap metal's value and how to identify one metal from another. If we saw that someone had discarded an electric motor or an appliance, we would collect it with the pickup truck that Pop always owned. We accumulated a pile of "junk" in the backyard and needed to separate the copper from the iron and the aluminum. I loved cleaning the electric motors because they had a massive amount of insulation that needed to be burned off, and the blue and green colors of the burning copper were magnificent.

When we were ready to cash it in, we would take each pile separately into Glosser Brothers Scrap Yard where it was weighed and valued and where we were paid by the pound. The assayer would carefully examine a load to make sure he was paying for copper and not a mass of rocks hidden at the bottom of the load. If you had a large enough load, he would weigh the whole truck before and after delivery and pay the weight difference. It was great fun, and we made a few bucks in the process.

On one occasion, my dad and brother Dick were standing in line at the scrap yard with a box of copper waiting to have it weighed. A big, burly guy came in with his box and slammed it down in front of them. Dad said politely, "We are in line here," and the big guy said, "God helps those that help themselves." Dad made it clear that wasn't an acceptable answer by saying, "If you don't move that goddamned box, you'll need God's help." The big guy quickly backed down by saying, "I was only kidding." He shifted his box to its proper place in line.

Pop teaching me to change the oil. Everything was an opportunity to learn something new.

Football at Berkley Cemetery

We played football nearly every day. It was usually two-handed touch, but on weekends, we played tackle. As mentioned previously, our yard was flat due to my dad's monumental effort to keep us kids in our yard. When he purchased the property, he brought in hundreds of loads of soil, and because of his accomplished mission, our yard became the mecca for all sports. We played baseball, basketball, and football so frequently that grass seldom had a chance to grow to maturity. The other advantage was that our yard looked like a football field, albeit smaller. The playable area was probably 100' by 50', the perfect shape for a miniature football field.

There were also two other locations where we would play if other neighborhoods wanted to join the fun. The Berkley Hill Cemetery had a section where only a few burials had taken place; therefore, we only had to contend with a scattering of headstones on the playing field. The other field was behind the aluminum factory where shards of dumped scrap metal could lay under the surface at any given spot. Getting tackled onto an aluminum shaving could result in a laceration and resulting stitches. Since nobody wanted to play there or at the cemetery, our yard was the default football field until we entered junior high school.

We mostly played pickup games depending on who would show up. We all knew each player's strengths and weaknesses, so if someone showed up late, some quick trading would take place on the spot to even out the odds. It wasn't unusual for a player to be traded more than once in the same game. The football games were hard-fought, and while they often ended with minor injuries, seldom was there anything that required a run to the hospital. We kept score for those games but never thought about keeping track of the season since the teams became scrambled from week-to-week. I truly loved playing pickup football.

The Day I Almost Killed Galen

Our gang was playing some game in our backyard when a sudden thunderstorm struck with such fierceness that we ran to our one-car garage attached to our house. The garage door, a one-piece wooden type, was open, and everyone crowded in and immediately began to break out the myriad of toys and bikes there. It was on this day that Galen was with us. He was new to the neighborhood and was friendly and well-liked by everyone. He was older by a year and Asian, which made him exciting and different to us.

The rain was slanting into the garage, and we were all getting wet. I knew of a trick where I could put the garage door halfway down, thereby extending the protected area by a few feet and creating a smaller space for the rain to enter. Since my arms couldn't reach the garage door pull rope, I used a garden hoe to lower the door part way. I could then quickly put the hoe under the garage door to prop it open. I had done it before with no problems, but this time, unfortunately, as I was pushing the garage door with the hoe when it slipped. At that exact moment, Galen was riding on an old metal toy tractor that was too small for him and was having a good time until the hoe's sharp edge hit him on the top of his head. To this day, I don't know how that didn't kill him. I remember Galen screaming, holding the top of his head, with blood running between his fingers as he ran out into the rain to his home. It was so traumatic that it remains a nightmare that I still have on occasion. Galen knew that it had been an accident and never held a grudge toward me resulting from the incident.

Our Basement in Bad Weather

Our basement was our playground, especially in bad weather. We used the coal furnace as a foundry in our attempt to make knives. We created a shooting range for BB guns at targets torn from catalog pages taped to a cardboard box full of towels so we could catch and recycle the BBs. We also made plastic model ship kits, would float them in a large tub of water, and then would also shoot them full of BBs. After sinking them, we would raise the models, cover the holes with Scotch tape, and repeat the process. Our wise parents eventually decided not to buy us the plastic models since all we did was shoot them full of holes.

Sometimes, brother Dick would make a model house or building from a cardboard box, carefully cutting out windows and doors to make it look realistic. He then would secure it on one side of a stationary tub, light it on fire, and have a bucket of water sitting on the top of the other side. Dick would siphon a small hose so that a stream of water would come out to fight the blaze. It was nip and tuck, and sometimes he wasn't able to save too much of the house, depending on how long it took the fire company to get there. Great imaginations!

"Bricks" were also a favorite rainy-day toy. Bricks are a wooden predecessor to Legos. They came in two colors, yellow and red, along with a couple of different sizes. We had a large box of these bricks from an old set (many of which had shrunk and discolored over time) and a newer set, which we still call *new* despite their being over sixty years old. We all made brick race cars and entered them into a competition governed by Dick on an oval-shaped rug. The race cars had different sized engines: most had a V8, but some had straight-six if the car's design wouldn't accommodate a larger engine. We all felt that

Dick would run a fair race, but we pretty much knew the outcome before the checkered flag would fall.

When my mom moved out of our Columbia Street home, I salvaged a small box of bricks. Years later, when I had children of my own, I showed them how we played with bricks and had my son and daughter build cars. We had a great time. My grandkids preferred Legos and, disappointingly, were bored with the bricks.

In the foreground are three racecars made of bricks, built by my son Will, my daughter Becky, and me. The ones on the left and center sport V8 engines. The one on the right is a mid-engine variety (I'm guessing). In the background is a six-gun battleship prepared for action.

Wounds and Scars

We all had many battle scars from growing up. It was just a normal part of childhood. Doris broke her toe dancing just before she graduated from high school. Dick burnt his hand, and Bruce put his front teeth through his bottom lip as he was climbing on circus equipment at the Fire Hall Jubilee. Wayne has one scar on his face after kids shook him out of a tree and another from falling into a gutter by the road while playing "Kick the Can." He hit his face on the macadam of the road, knocking himself silly, and was carried home by the other kids. Wayne also hit Bruce in the forehead with a metal bracket that also resulted in a trip to the emergency room. I have multiple scars on my left knee from separate incidents, but strangely none on my right knee. To this day, I have a black scar on my left thigh that resulted from an elementary school sword fight with sharp lead pencils. Touché! Since Many of these wounds resulted in trips to the emergency room, the Gregory's were not strangers at the hospital.

Sammy vs. Pixie – the Bout of the Century

Seldom did a scuffle get out of hand in those days. Oh, there were plenty of quarrels, which led to a punch being thrown. Two guys would get into a wrestling match, and whoever got on top first basically won. Nonetheless, something happened

one day between Sammy and Pixie that came down to an
outright challenge to meet behind the aluminum factory at high
noon for fisticuffs until the winner drew blood. I know that
sounds a little dramatic, but when you are ten years old, the
drama was real, and the stakes were high. Sammy was an older
neighbor in the same grade as my twin brothers. Although
Pixie was an odd nickname for a young man, he was a pretty
tough and not someone to be regarded lightly. He was the same
age as Sammy, came from a different neighborhood, but only
lived about two blocks away from Columbia Street.

I don't know what caused the fight, but it was rare for
one to be declared. Sammy turned up a few minutes early
accompanied by an entourage of supporters and curiosity
seekers and was boasting that Pixie wouldn't show. When Pixie
showed up about 5 minutes later with his crowd of friends,
Sammy looked a little sick. It seemed for a few minutes that
this party might turn into a gang fight as both sides lined up
against each other. The musical *West Side Story* was all the
rage since it had just debuted on Broadway, and its melodies
were playing in my head as both sides squared-off. Then
Sammy and Pixie started yapping and insulting each other, and
I finally learned that the fight was, of course, about a girl. Ugh!
I certainly wasn't going to get my ass kicked in a gang fight
over a stupid girl.

As I recall, and the rest of the event gets a little fuzzy as I was quickly losing interest, Pixie called Sammy a chicken, and that is when the fists started flying. There were several hard hits, and then they fell wrestling on the ground, quickly becoming covered in mud. I honestly don't know who won as I had slowly backed away toward my bicycle. Suddenly, the fight was abruptly over, and both sides considered the matter closed.

Cub Scout – Cooking Badge

Cub Scouts introduced me to new neighbors and skills. I was the first in my family to join the Scouts, so I had no idea of what to expect. There were meetings to attend, pledges to memorize, and dues to pay. The sessions were somewhat interesting, but the more appealing opportunities were all geared to camping: how to build fires, how to make a lean-to, and how to cook your meals. All of this came with the *Cub Scout Manual* that allowed for quick advancement, which seemed very appealing compared to elementary school's drudgery.

We would go on day hikes in the area woods where we tested our skills. I can remember my mom teaching me to make scrambled eggs the day before a hike where cooking a meal was required. Making the eggs over a gas stove is one thing but cooking eggs over a wet campfire is quite different. It seemed like it took a half-hour to cook those eggs, but I was determined to eat them to get my cooking badge. So, I wolfed down the half-cooked scrambled eggs and cold uncooked diced potatoes. The hike back to my home was not pleasant.

Many years later when I had children of my own, I became a Cub Scout leader, and I'm very proud to say that my son Will was an excellent scout in my den. Will eventually became an Eagle Scout. There was one memorable campout at a state park, and, of course, it rained. The morning chores were to make campfires and cook your own breakfast. My breakfast was, as you guessed it, scrambled eggs, and my nightmares quickly returned because they were awful, and I ended up throwing them away. I kept telling my son that he had better start moving or he was going to be hungry. However, my son always moved at his own methodical pace and proceeded to make the most beautiful stack of pancakes that I have ever seen. I mean, there was a pad of melting butter on the top and syrup running down the sides. You could have taken a picture of the stack and used it on pancake mix packaging. I want to think that I taught Will all he knows. I wish I had taught him to share!

Mom's Infinite Wisdom and Influence on Our Us

Mom had several phrases that she always offered every day before she sent us off to school. Of course, we often teased Mom for proposing these little pearls of wisdom, but their true value has become much clearer and more appreciated as time wore.

"Walk the straight and narrow path." As a kid, I never knew just what it meant. It originally had a religious meaning, and the path is often mentioned in the Bible. Walking the straight and narrow path undoubtedly means that the way to happiness doesn't vary and meander – stay on target and don't be swayed by other temptations. Easier said than done.

"Set your goals." The higher you place your life goals, the more you'll achieve them. Anything is possible, but you need to know where you are going to achieve your goals. A life without dreams is much more difficult because you don't know when you've made progress.

"Aim high." Mom would say, but I had no identified goals at all until I completed high school. After that, my dreams grew exponentially while I was in college. Our father's unexpected passing during my senior year of college served as a multiplier, and my goals increased significantly. Even lofty goals are often swiftly achievable, so it is essential to think out where you want to go with your goals and how you'll feel once you achieve them. Make sure that you set them high enough that you won't feel let down once you get them, which can happen if you don't aim high.

"Buckle down." When Mom gave this advice, I laughed and tightened my belt another notch, at which point she would laugh and swat me out the door. What "buckle down" really means is to work hard to achieve whatever you are seeking. Life is a wonderful treat if you live it to its fullest, but if you are just along for the ride, it can be a bore. I have absolutely no patience for people who drift through life—what a waste.

"You can't turn back the clock." Of all of Mom's mantras, this is the one I have taken most seriously. In her later years, I asked her to explain this one. She said, "You can't turn back the clock to another time. Enjoy all of life's pleasures and be happy. You can't wish you had done something differently. Think about what you say and do, be satisfied with what you are, and what you have accomplished."

Mom with the twins and Dick in our backyard.

Our Columbia Street Home

By any measure, the children in our family enjoyed an extraordinary upbringing. Our parents instilled an excellent combination of love, support, curiosity, creativity, and common sense in each of us. We were encouraged to create our entertainment, and despite the age gaps that separated us, it was those invented activities that are the most cherished memories. Imagination, often sparked by brother Dick, was the source of inspiration in our home.

Our parents weren't wealthy, but we children never felt inadequate or the sting of being poor. Our father dropped out of high school to get a job in the steel mill, and our mother had a high-school education. Yet, we were always encouraged to aim high and study hard, which would help us to achieve our dreams.

Our family certainly had its share of arguments, some trivial and others more substantive, but underlying all was a core foundation of love that was pervasive.

So how did our parents do it?

Pop and Mom visit Penn State University where Bruce and Wayne were enrolled (circa 1964).

Billie Maxine Lawhead was the 10th of 12 children. She came from a financially successful family in Windber that lost everything in The Great Depression. George Alvin Gregory, Jr., was the third of four boys in a family whose roots went back to the early history of the iron and steel industry in Johnstown. Both families were rightfully proud and accomplished.

Billie Maxine Lawhead

George and Maxine met in the local minstrel shows where Mom played the banjo, and Pop played the trumpet and sang. They were young and in love. They got married on May 17, 1931, which meant The Great Depression had a long way to go before it ended. The Depression caused them tremendous hardship in those early years, and in many ways, left deep and painful scars on their lives.

A page from Maxine's scrapbook is dated May 17, 1931.

The "little house" in Old Westmont.

In the early years of their marriage, they lived in a cramped two-room house known as the "little house" in the back yard of Pop's parents' home. When they could finally afford their own home, they found a lot located on a former pasture of Mr. Berkley's Farm. It was a section of town that became known as Berkley Hills.

Pop home from work.

Mom with Dick and Doris

Dick breaking ground for the house on Berkley Hills.

When Mom and Pop finally moved into the house on Columbia Street in 1941, they had two small children, and soon the twins were on the way. The US was entering World War II, and steelworkers were essential to the war effort.

These are some of the circumstances that explain the great pride and herculean effort it took to transform their home on Columbia Street and the backyard into a desired destination for their kids and the friends they invited to play there.

Mom and Pop showed tremendous resiliency in responding to the many complex challenges in their lives. The result was they provided a warm and inviting home where imaginations thrived, and love was evident every single day.

Our parents instilled a sense of curiosity and a deep interest in history that has stayed with their children and grandchildren. Visiting many Civil War and Revolutionary War battlefields over the years was the best American history lesson. Pop could make the battlefield come alive with his narration of what took place where most would only see trees and fields. Likewise, exploring the ruins of old iron furnaces is how we learned about the industrial revolution. We were taught to envision how the iron furnace process worked, from the mines in the hillside charging the top of the furnace to tapping the molten iron at the bottom. That is the kind of education that sticks with children and passes to future generations. Mom and

Pop also instilled a sense of patriotism, and we were very proud that brothers Dick, Bruce, and Wayne all served in the US Navy.

Whether we were fishing at state parks or simply having a picnic, there were always subtle lessons and patient advice. Our parents were very much involved in our lives, even while giving us the freedom to explore our world. It was a great environment they created that we didn't fully appreciate until we had children of our own.

Our backyard with Dick in the commander's tent while Bruce and Wayne entertained the girls.

Mom and Pop intended to create a safe play area in our yard, and they succeeded with homemade swings, teeter-totter, tents, basketball hoops, etc., and our yard tended to be the place where the entire "Berkley Hills" neighborhood gathered. Mom and Pop had gone to great lengths to make our home a destination for the neighborhood kids. Imagination blossomed at our house on Columbia Street. Glenda Gindlesberger said in her comments on her friend Sam Kelly's obituary, "…My memory of Sam was playing barefoot and happy in the Gregory's backyard."

The End

\

Portrait of a happy kid! Then came the teenage years!

About the authors

Dr. James R. Gregory currently resides in Bradenton, Florida. He is married to Evelyn, and they have two grown children, Becky and Will. Becky is married to David Friedman, and they have two children Charlotte and Maxwell. Dr. Gregory has written numerous business books about corporate branding. His first fictional book is called *Small Fortunes* is available on Amazon's Kindle Vella platform. For more information about Dr. Gregory's business consulting services, please see the website www.NYLAQ.com his email address is jgregory@NYLAQ.com.

Richard A. Gregory currently resides near Johnstown, Pennsylvania. He is married to Sara, and they have four grown children, two boys and two girls, Douglas, Leslie, Kirk, and Allison and nine grandchildren and three great grandchildren. Over the last 20 years in retirement, he researched and authored the historical fiction *The Bosses Club* and produced an illustrated booklet *The Great Johnstown Flood of 1889 (the untold story)*. His website is at www.thebossesclub.com and his email address is rgreg.cbm@gmail.com

Bruce Gregory is retired and lives with his wife "Jess" in Leland, North Carolina. They have two sons: Todd and Bret. Todd and Misha have two sons: Andrew and Ryan. Bret and Kristen have a son Mathew and daughter Reagan.

Wayne Gregory and his wife Lee Ann are retired and live in Prescott, Arizona. Son Mike and wife Cheryl live in Discovery Bay, California and have two daughters in college.

Author's note: Many of the names have been changed to protect the innocent. Some of the narratives have been exaggerated or altered somewhat from the actual events to make them more interesting. This story represents a snapshot of the 1950s and 60s in Middle America. If there are factual errors or corrections, please let me know for future editions. For questions or comments please contact James Gregory at the email address below:
jgregory@NYLAQ.com